THEOLOGYGRAMS

Theology explained in diagrams

RICH WYLD

DARTON·LONGMAN+TODD

First published in Great Britain in 2014 by
Darton, Longman and Todd Ltd
1 Spencer Court
140-142 Wandsworth High Street
London SW18 4JJ

ISBN 978-0-232-53076-6

A catalogue record for this book is available from the British Library

Designed and phototypeset by Judy Linard
Printed and bound Printed in Turkey by Imak Offset

CONTENTS

INTRODUCTION

Psalm 1 suggests that it is wise to meditate on the law of the Lord but foolish to sit in the seat of mockery. This book comes dangerously close to doing both, so a little introduction might be handy. On the one hand, these diagrams offer a visual way of thinking about theology. They move from Old Testament to the New, through some historical figures and up to modern-day questions about the Bible, ethics and so on. On the other hand, this is quite a silly book about some quite serious stuff, but the intention is never to mock or belittle God, theology, the Bible or the Church.

As this collection is random at best, where a Bible verse is given I'd encourage the reader to look up the passage in question; each diagram is only a commentary, and so the passage will have more to say than can be captured in one image. Indeed, I hope that for the whole book, some of these diagrams will inspire (or irritate?) you to look further into some subject or other that grabs you.

At best, the sillier side of the book might help us not to take too seriously our human efforts to explain things. The importance of this has something to do with human nature, but as I haven't worked out how to put that into a diagram I won't say any more about it here. At the very least, I hope this book is mildly diverting. Beyond that, I hope it might spark fresh questions and thoughts. Beyond THAT, I hope it will be a bestseller. But I'll settle for mildly diverting.

1
OLD TESTAMENT

The Old Testament: let us start at the very beginning. The Old Testament is a vast and rich collection of diverse writings, whose breadth and depth is somewhat undermined by the scant attention given to it in this book. There are two reasons for this; some of the material does not lend itself to visual representation, but the main reason is that I don't know it as well as I should. I do feel honesty is a good thing. What we have are a few diagrams with which to dip our theological toes into the biblical seas. Genesis is the first of the first five books, called the Pentateuch, which collectively tell of the origins of Israel, the great Exodus and the Law of Moses. Among other things. The Psalms are like poems of praise and prayer that seem to convey every imaginable human emotion to God. Ecclesiastes forms part of the wisdom tradition, though it might represent a slightly odd phase in that heritage when compared to Proverbs. Isaiah, Amos and Jonah are all prophets, whose task was to bring God's words to steer the people in the right direction, and also to announce God's promise of restoration when things went badly.

FLAT-PACK CREATION

You will need:

- Screwdriver
- Allen keys
- Power over time and space

Step 1: Lay all the pieces out on the floor. They will appear like a formless void. Don't worry: begin by separating light (L) from dark (D).

Step 2: Now take the sky (S) and fix it between the waters (W1 and W2).

Step 3: Separate the lower waters (W1) using the earth. Attach the seed-bearing plants, fruit trees (P1) and other vegetation. Use the allen key if needed.

Step 4: Attach the lights (L1 and L2), making sure that the larger one is in the day and the smaller in the night. Attach stars freely.

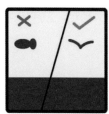

Step 5: Add sea creatures and birds. Ensure the fish go in the sea and the birds in the air. Use diagram for help.

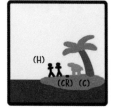

Step 6: Add cattle (C), wild animals and creeping things (CR). Add humankind (H). These can be tricky so use a hammer if necessary.

Step 7: Your creation is fully assembled. Relax!

GENESIS 1-11

I'm not going to go into the inevitable questions about history and science and things, mainly because I have no wisdom to offer on that subject. What this diagram shows are some nice parallels in the way the material has been arranged before and after the flood (chapters 6-8). The flood is a key turning point in the story, and that fact alone should justify the amount of songs about Noah's Ark.

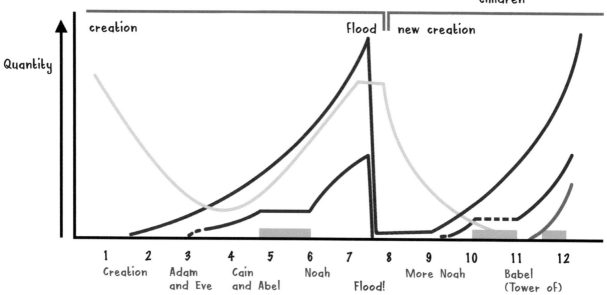

Structure of the 'Pre-history' up to Abraham

Legend:
- Living things
- Rebellion/disobedience
- Genealogies
- Languages
- Related songs for children

Quantity

creation — Flood — new creation

1	2	3	4	5	6	7	8	9	10	11	12

Creation — Adam and Eve — Cain and Abel — Noah — Flood! — More Noah — Babel (Tower of)

NOAH'S ARK

Noah's Ark

Genesis 6.11–22 (P)

Cain's

Owner's Workshop Manual

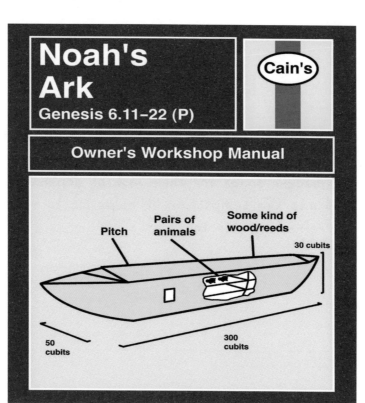

Pitch

Pairs of animals

Some kind of wood/reeds

30 cubits

50 cubits

300 cubits

PSALM 150

I've sometimes noticed debate between people who like modern worship songs in Church, and people who like more traditional hymns. Sometimes, there is a temptation to knock modern songs for their lack of sophistication in the lyric department. As I fall into this temptation, it helps me to recall this psalm which is, in the end, refreshingly to the point.

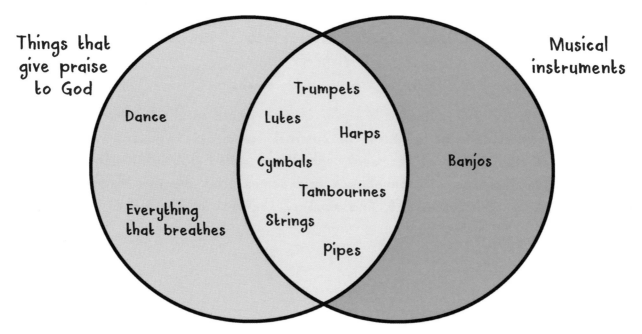

Things that give praise to God

Musical instruments

Dance

Trumpets
Lutes
Harps
Cymbals
Tambourines
Strings
Pipes

Banjos

Everything that breathes

I actually play the banjo, just in case you were offended.

ECCLESIASTES PIE CHART, PART 1

Ecclesiastes is by any reckoning a fairly gloomy phase in the wisdom tradition, though it can actually be a source of comfort for people who can relate to the Teacher (the author of the book, sometimes called Qoholeth). Other wisdom texts include Proverbs, Wisdom, Sirach and James. This diagram visualises the basic thrust of Ecclesiastes 1.14. And most of the rest of the book.

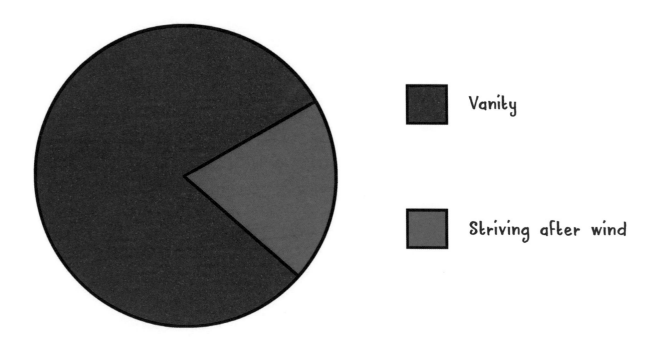

Vanity

Striving after wind

ISAIAH 55.9

They say a picture can say 1000 words. Isaiah is quite long, so the odd diagram may make it more manageable. As a piece of prophetic literature, each section of Isaiah maintains a plea to return to God, though this part of the book offers a sense of promise that the exiled people of God will return home. This image simply reminds the reader of who God is, and why it is worth looking to God.

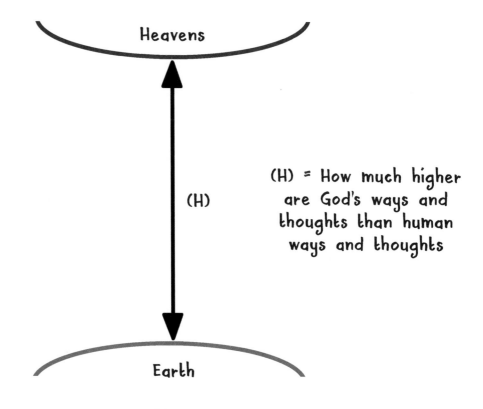

(H) = How much higher are God's ways and thoughts than human ways and thoughts

ISAIAH 58

In a nutshell

Ditto really, though with a harsher edge.

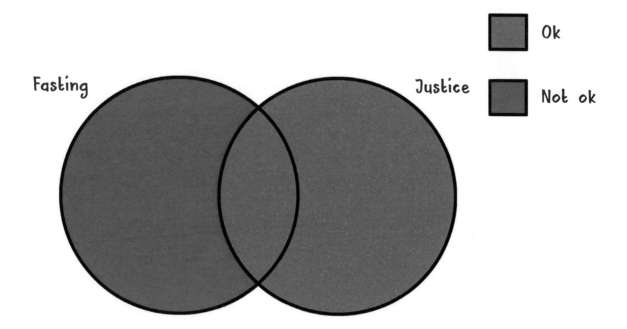

Fasting

Justice

Ok

Not ok

AMOS 5
In a nutshell

A theme is emerging here. Amos (one of the twelve minor prophets) contains a similar plea to Isaiah. Following these two, it would be easy to be harsh on those who fast or play music in church, but I can easily imagine the words of a modern-day prophet: 'Away with the colours of your pie charts! I will not look upon your Venn diagrams! But let justice flow like a river.'

This is actually quite serious.

Music 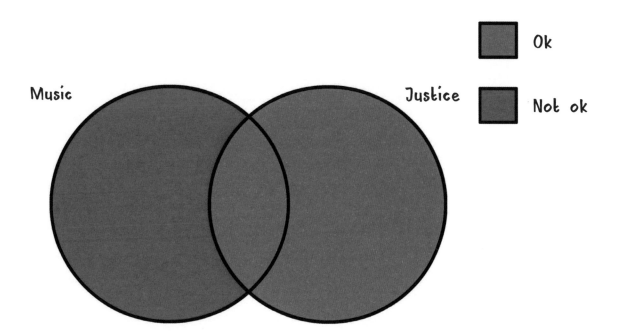 Justice

Ok

Not ok

ECCLESIASTES PIE CHART, PART II

I thought I'd jump back to Ecclesiastes 3 with this one, just to mix things up. This passage is actually quite well known. It has a highly poetic rhythm to it, which I have essentially dismantled in a lurid pie chart.

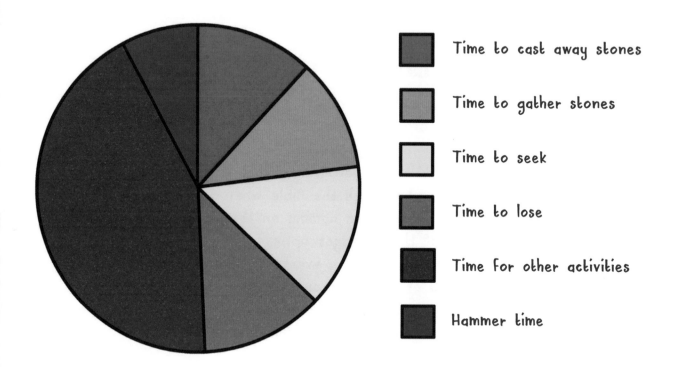

Time to cast away stones

Time to gather stones

Time to seek

Time to lose

Time for other activities

Hammer time

THE LIFE CYCLE OF A MESSIANIC TEXT

To get this one you really need to have a look at each passage, which I admit might make this diagram a little self-defeating. What it aims to show is that you can draw a kind of thread through the Bible when an idea reoccurs, in this case the image of the Son of Man coming on the clouds of heaven. This image comes back in each of the passages opposite, and it shows that at successive points, people are interpreting events through the image first found in Daniel. This could be said of Isaiah 53 or Zechariah 9, and in each case the point has perhaps less to do with predictions being fulfilled, and more to do with a strong sense of theological continuity. Which is another way of saying that God is faithful.

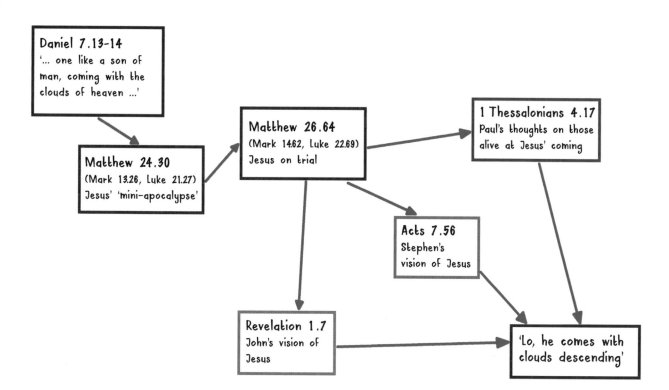

Daniel 7.13-14
'... one like a son of man, coming with the clouds of heaven ...'

Matthew 24.30
(Mark 13.26, Luke 21.27)
Jesus' 'mini-apocalypse'

Matthew 26.64
(Mark 14.62, Luke 22.69)
Jesus on trial

1 Thessalonians 4.17
Paul's thoughts on those alive at Jesus' coming

Acts 7.56
Stephen's vision of Jesus

Revelation 1.7
John's vision of Jesus

'Lo, he comes with clouds descending'

JONAH'S MOOD-O-METER

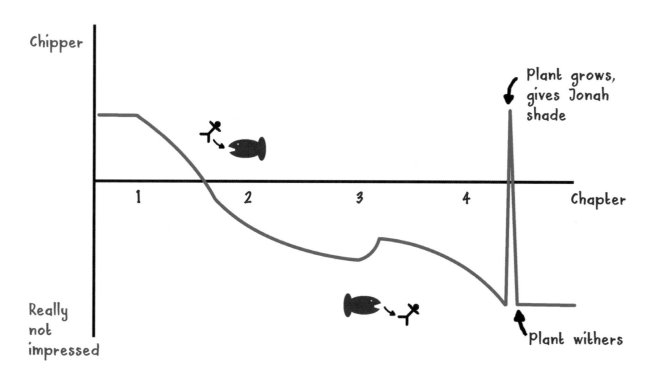

Chipper

Really
not
impressed

Chapter

1   2   3   4

Plant grows,
gives Jonah
shade

Plant withers

2
GOSPELS

This section is a blend of two things really; some fairly daft diagrams which relate to the teachings and actions of Jesus, and others which outline some more complex ideas, especially surrounding the diversity of the accounts of Jesus' life. There are four Gospels, though three of these (Matthew, Mark and Luke) are referred to as the synoptic Gospels. This is because they are all quite similar, whereas John has many differences: the timing of events, the detail of the teaching, some of the concepts used, and the apparent lack of a Last Supper. However, all the Gospels do focus on the person of Jesus, and on his death and resurrection. The differences between each version can help to build a more multi-dimensional picture, and need not always be seen as a problem. It's worth spending time to look at each account on its own terms, before supplementing it with the others.

This introduction has been rather serious. Erm ... sorry about that. I hope it was interesting.

STORIES OF JESUS' BIRTH

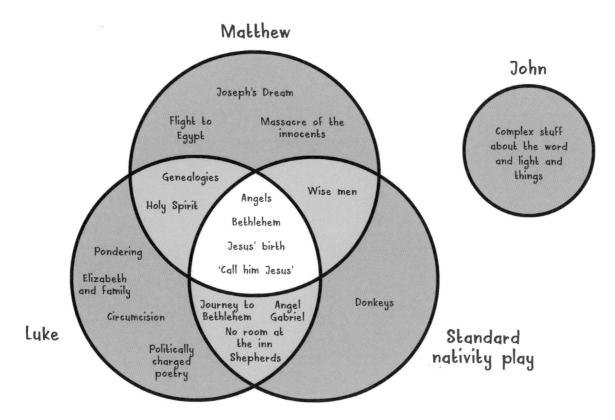

Matthew

John

Joseph's Dream

Flight to Egypt

Massacre of the innocents

Complex stuff about the word and light and things

Genealogies

Holy Spirit

Angels

Bethlehem

Jesus' birth

'Call him Jesus'

Wise men

Pondering

Elizabeth and family

Circumcision

Journey to Bethlehem

Angel Gabriel

No room at the inn

Shepherds

Donkeys

Luke

Politically charged poetry

Standard nativity play

QUALITY OF WINE DURING A WEDDING

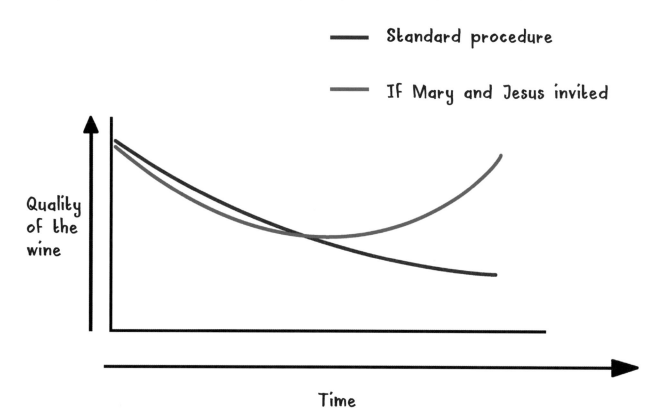

Standard procedure

If Mary and Jesus invited

Quality of the wine

Time

JESUS' SERMON IN LUKE 4

This sermon has all the hallmarks of snatching defeat from the jaws of victory. Jesus is wowing the crowd, but then causes a minor riot by mentioning two seemingly obscure stories about the widow of Zaraphath (1 Kings 17) and Namaan the Syrian (2 Kings 5). In actual fact, these two stories undercut any expectations (which would have been there) that his task was to lead nationalistic revolution, because these two figures were so-called outsiders. While Jesus does focus on his own community, the seeds for a much wider message are being sown.

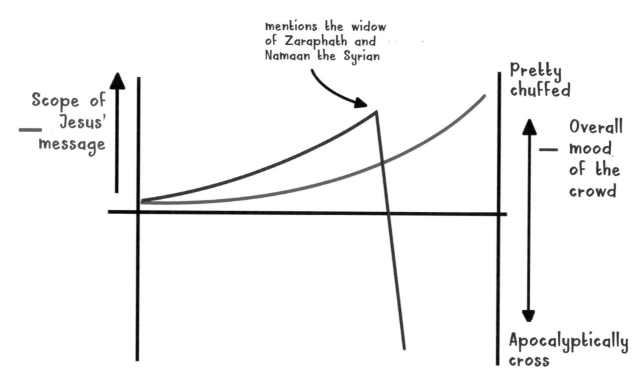

mentions the widow
of Zaraphath and
Namaan the Syrian

Scope of
Jesus'
message

Pretty
chuffed

Overall
mood
of the
crowd

Apocalyptically
cross

ESCHATOLOGICAL REVERSAL

First things first, 'eschatology' refers to the study of 'the end', but this doesn't just mean the end of the world. It can refer to a decisive moment in time, when something ends and something else begins. A lot of OT passages look forward to a reversal of fortune coming through a decisive act of God, and a number of NT passages declare that this is happening in Jesus.

See: Luke 1.52-53 (Magnificat)
    Luke 6.20,24
    Corinthians 1.27-28
    James 1.9-10
    Revelation 2.9

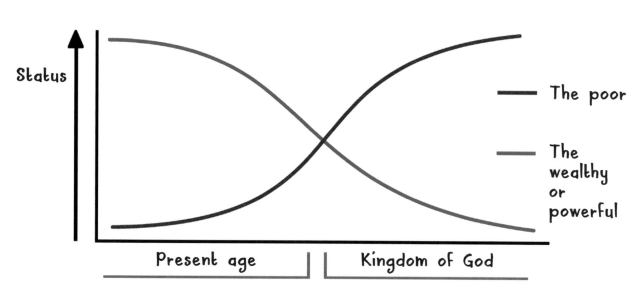

IF JESUS USED CHARTS INSTEAD OF PARABLES, 1

Matthew 7.24-27

This story is of course not about building houses, but is an image for what it means to follow the words of Jesus. There are some places in the world where it is actually better to build your house on sand, and so Bible translators are faced with a tricky dilemma: should they flip this story round so it makes sense in those places, or hold on to the actual image Jesus used? There will be a diagram about this later on.

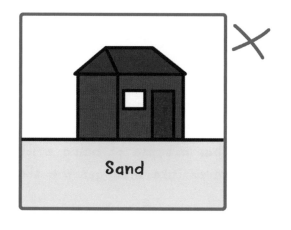

Sand

Not OK

Rock

OK

IF JESUS USED CHARTS INSTEAD OF PARABLES, 2

Luke 12.16-21

This parable argues that the accumulation of stuff is ultimately futile, but is also deceptive. Luke's Gospel has been singled out as the one that speaks most about wealth and poverty, though it also has a sense of being written to appeal to people of 'high standing'. But however Luke arranges the stories, these challenging words remain very much there.

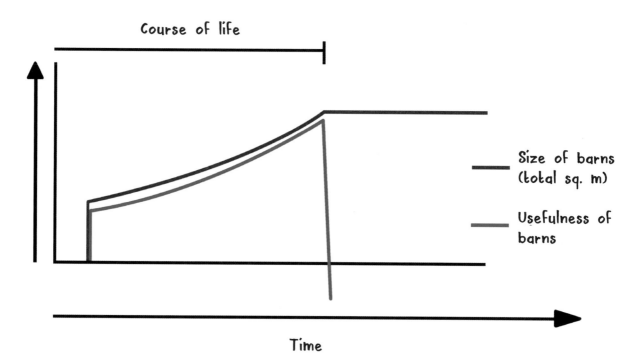

Course of life

Size of barns
(total sq. m)

Usefulness of
barns

Time

43

PARABLES IN THE SYNOPTIC GOSPELS

If you've never seen a book outlining the parallels between the Gospels, they look nothing like this. But the basic idea is to outline which bits are found where, and that might help deepen our sense of what each author is trying to tell us individually. Having said that, I'm not 100% sure what this diagram does show us, but you get the idea.

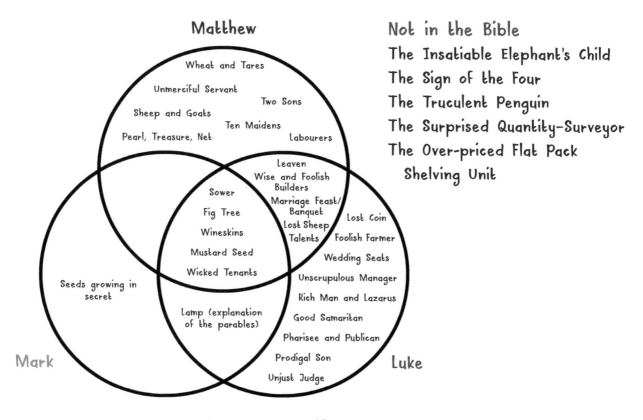

Matthew

Wheat and Tares

Unmerciful Servant

Two Sons

Sheep and Goats

Ten Maidens

Pearl, Treasure, Net

Labourers

Leaven

Wise and Foolish Builders

Sower

Marriage Feast/ Banquet

Fig Tree

Lost Sheep

Lost Coin

Wineskins

Talents

Foolish Farmer

Mustard Seed

Wedding Seats

Wicked Tenants

Unscrupulous Manager

Seeds growing in secret

Rich Man and Lazarus

Lamp (explanation of the parables)

Good Samaritan

Pharisee and Publican

Prodigal Son

Mark

Unjust Judge

Luke

Not in the Bible
The Insatiable Elephant's Child
The Sign of the Four
The Truculent Penguin
The Surprised Quantity-Surveyor
The Over-priced Flat Pack
    Shelving Unit

IF JESUS USED CHARTS INSTEAD OF PARABLES, 3

Matthew 13

This is one of the few parables where the disciples ask for an explanation, and Jesus responds by explaining. The irony of this diagram is that Jesus describes how the different soil represents the different conditions of those who hear God's word (the seed), and that each condition goes on to shape their response to the word. None of that is contained in this diagram, and had Jesus had it to hand, it would therefore have done nothing to help his disciples. Sorry about that.

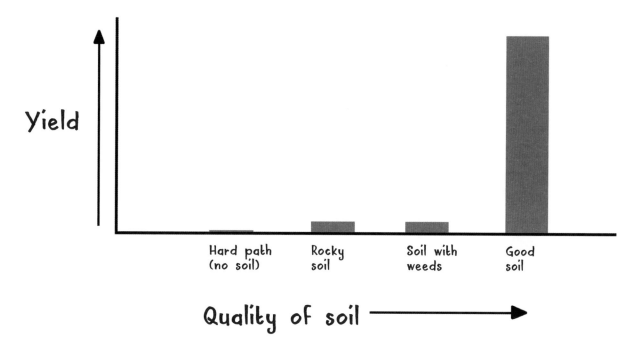

IF JESUS USED CHARTS INSTEAD OF PARABLES, 4

Matthew 25.14-30

If I'm honest, I sometimes find this parable quite difficult. It talks about the importance of using what we have for God, but that is often quite difficult, as illustrated by my performance at Monopoly. My own view is that Jesus is not talking about failure through fear or weakness, but about complacency. The problem occurs when we hide our talents because we do not recognise that the world needs them. But I'm getting too preachy so I'll shut up.

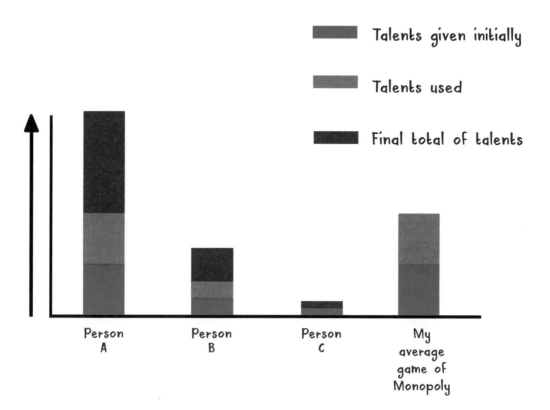

Talents given initially
Talents used
Final total of talents

Person A

Person B

Person C

My average game of Monopoly

49

IF JESUS USED CHARTS INSTEAD OF PARABLES, 5

Luke 10.25-37

Jesus says that the greatest commands are to love God and our neighbour. Someone asks him who the neighbour actually is. In response, Jesus tells the story of the Good Samaritan, though he could have equally used this chart. Having said that, I am in no way wishing to correct Jesus on his technique, and I strongly suspect that this diagram would have had much less staying power. In fact, ignore this diagram and read the passage. It's much better.

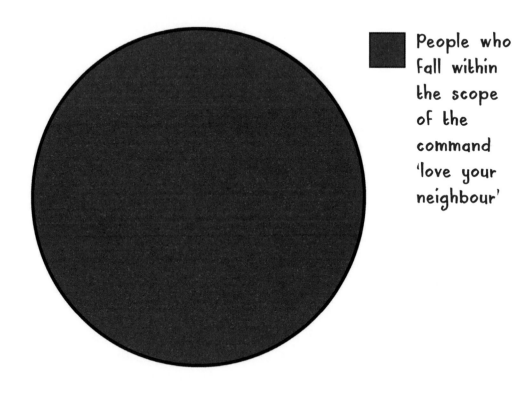

People who fall within the scope of the command 'love your neighbour'

WHAT JESUS SAID AT THE LAST SUPPER

There are probably two traditions about what Jesus said at the last supper, one drawn on by Mark and Matthew, and the other by Paul (esteemed author of 1 Corinthians) and Luke. Observing the subtle differences can enrich the overall sense of what Jesus meant. John, however, raises all sorts of questions. The gathering of John 13-17 has important elements in common with the other Gospels, but the timing is different, and crucially there are no words relating to the bread and wine. What is going on? Will this book explain? No. Sorry. But as a starter, a good theory is that John has shifted the timing of his story so that Jesus dies at the same time that the Passover lambs are sacrificed, reinforcing his point about Jesus being the lamb of God. This doesn't explain why John has nothing about the bread and wine, but it begins to show how differences in detail might prove to be illuminating.

			This is my body	That is for you	Do this in remembrance of me	This cup		Is the new covenant in my blood			Do this, as often as you drink it, in remembrance of me		
1 Corinthians			This is my body	That is for you	Do this in remembrance of me	This cup		Is the new covenant in my blood			Do this, as often as you drink it, in remembrance of me		
Matthew		Take, eat	This is my body			Drink from it all of you		For this is my blood of the covenant	Which is poured out for many	For the forgiveness of sins		I tell you I will never again drink of this fruit of the vine until	that day when I drink it new with you in my Father's Kingdom
Mark		Take, eat	This is my body					This is my blood of the covenant	Which is poured out for many			Truly I tell you I will never again drink of the fruit of the vine until	that day when I drink it new with you in the Kingdom of God
Luke	Take this and divide it amongst yourselves	**	This is my body	Which is given for you	Do this in remembrance of me	This cup	*	Is the new covenant in my blood	*That is poured out for many			**For I tell you that from now on I will not drink of the fruit of the vine until	the Kingdom of God comes
John	If I, your Lord and teacher, have washed your feet, you also ought to wash one another's feet	?											

HOW TO DECIDE WHERE MARK'S GOSPEL ENDS

If you've never come across this question before then it may come as a bit of a shock. The problem is that the style of these verses differs quite a lot from the rest of the book, while some early manuscripts leave out these verses altogether. Typically, scholars cannot agree as to why this is the case, and the diagram opposite outlines some options. If you've never seen THE SHAWSHANK REDEMPTION, I can only apologise.

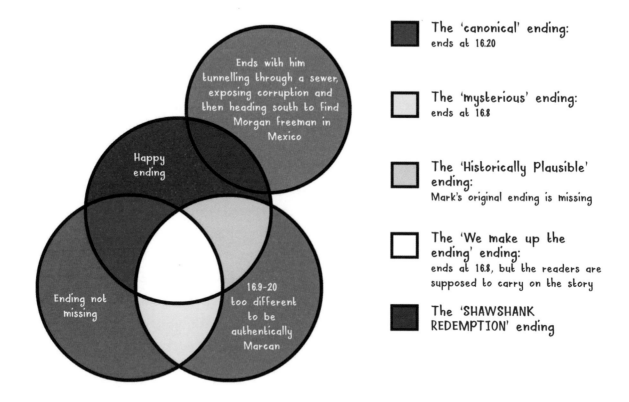

Ends with him tunnelling through a sewer, exposing corruption and then heading south to find Morgan Freeman in Mexico

Happy ending

Ending not missing

16.9-20 too different to be authentically Marcan

The 'canonical' ending: ends at 16.20

The 'mysterious' ending: ends at 16.8

The 'Historically Plausible' ending: Mark's original ending is missing

The 'We make up the ending' ending: ends at 16.8, but the readers are supposed to carry on the story

The 'SHAWSHANK REDEMPTION' ending

JESUS ASKS, 'WHO DO PEOPLE SAY THE SON OF MAN IS?'

This rather crucial moment is recorded in Matthew 16.13-20. Each possibility suggests some kind of significance for Jesus, but 'Christ' refers to the specific task of actually redeeming God's people, whereas the others point the way.

On a slightly related note, a friend of mine once pointed out that in theology, we can get a bit caught up on Jesus' first question (who do other people say I am?). However, Jesus follows this up with the more fundamental question: 'Who do you say I am?' I thought I'd share this with you as I find it quite helpful to remember whenever theology gets too abstract.

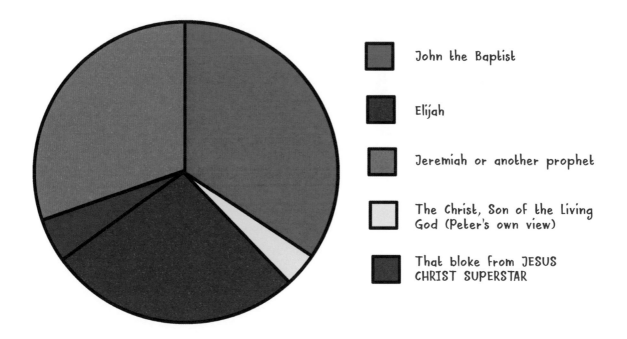

John the Baptist

Elijah

Jeremiah or another prophet

The Christ, Son of the Living
God (Peter's own view)

That bloke from JESUS
CHRIST SUPERSTAR

RESURRECTION APPEARANCES

Odd as it might sound, the Bible never describes Jesus' resurrection as such. But we are given two important bits of evidence. One is the empty tomb, and the other is the appearance of Jesus himself. Taken together, they point to the idea of a bodily resurrection, which is partly why the NT appearances of the risen Jesus differ somewhat from his more recent appearances in burnt toast.

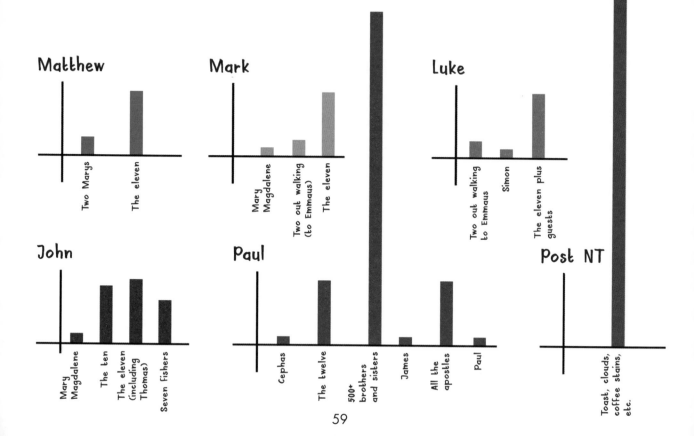

Matthew

- Two Marys
- The eleven

Mark

- Mary Magdalene
- Two out walking (to Emmaus)
- The eleven

Luke

- Two out walking to Emmaus
- Simon
- The eleven plus guests

John

- Mary Magdalene
- The ten
- The eleven (including Thomas)
- Seven fishers

Paul

- Cephas
- The twelve
- 500+ brothers and sisters
- James
- All the apostles
- Paul

Post NT

- Toast, clouds, coffee stains, etc.

ST PETER'S FAITH-O-METER

I personally find this rather encouraging. Peter (a.k.a. Simon or Cephas) had a particularly close relationship to Jesus, and became a foundation of the Church. Here are some of his exploits, which encompass the heights and depths of human faith.

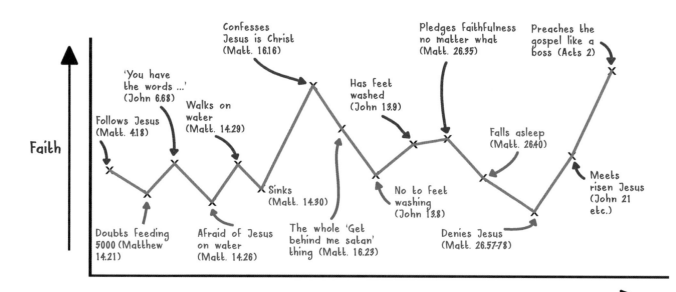

Faith

Confesses
Jesus is Christ
(Matt. 16.16)

'You have
the words ...'
(John 6.68)

Walks on
water
(Matt. 14.29)

Follows Jesus
(Matt. 4.18)

Has feet
washed
(John 13.9)

Pledges faithfulness
no matter what
(Matt. 26.35)

Preaches the
gospel like a
boss (Acts 2)

Falls asleep
(Matt. 26.40)

Doubts feeding
5000 (Matthew
14.21)

Afraid of Jesus
on water
(Matt. 14.26)

Sinks
(Matt. 14.30)

The whole 'Get
behind me satan'
thing (Matt. 16.23)

No to feet
washing
(John 13.8)

Denies Jesus
(Matt. 26.57-78)

Meets
risen Jesus
(John 21
etc.)

Time

3
THE REST OF THE NEW TESTAMENT

Like the Old, the New Testament is a collection of fairly diverse writings. After the Gospels, there is Acts, Luke's hotly anticipated sequel to the bestselling 'Luke'. There are many letters, some by Paul, some by others such as James and Peter. And then there's Revelation, which rounds everything off in a flurry of trumpets and dragons and thunderstorms. There's so much that could be said about why these documents were chosen, given that many others were circulating in the period when people were debating what should go in, but that's really a much more complex subject than I have space for here. But even though they now all sit under one roof, so to speak, this should not hide the fact that they are diverse and fascinating as a result.

The plan of action, as before, is to present some diagrams that pull out various ideas from a range of texts, though Corinthians and Revelation are perhaps a bit over-represented. This is because I got a bit over-enthusiastic while reading about them.

MISSION PLAN A
Acts 1-8

At the beginning of Acts, the risen Jesus gives his disciples a straightforward, if daunting, mission. As shown here, there is a sense of needing to step out, to move beyond the boundaries of the familiar world.

I recently moved to Dorset. It seems pretty unfamiliar right now.

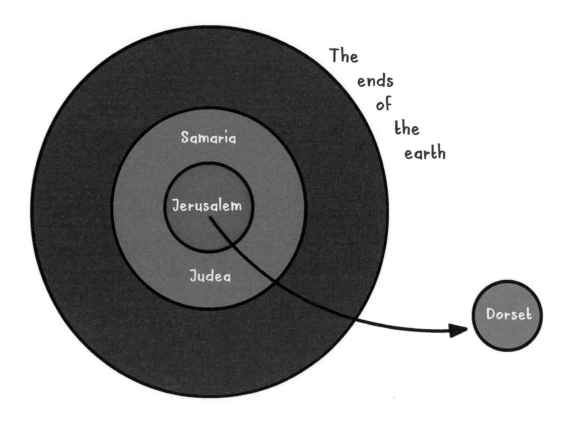

The
ends
of
the
earth

Samaria

Jerusalem

Judea

Dorset

PAUL'S MISSIONARY TUBE MAP

If Paul had undertaken his missionary journeys by underground, then no one in that region would have ever heard the Gospel, owing to the unwritten rule that you must never, ever talk to, or make eye contact with, another person on the tube. However, this is just a silly if topographical way of outlining where Paul went and when, as told by Luke in the book of Acts. Post Damascus road, Paul travels extensively to preach and nurture new churches. What this kind of map can do is to help locate Paul's letter-writing activity in the context of his movements, and that gives us some good clues as to things like what order he wrote the letters in.

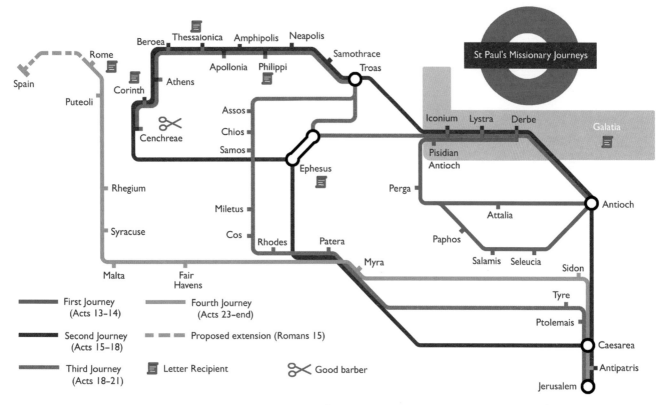

St Paul's Missionary Journeys

Spain

Rome

Puteoli

Rhegium

Syracuse

Malta

Fair
Havens

Beroea

Thessalonica

Amphipolis

Neapolis

Apollonia

Philippi

Samothrace

Troas

Athens

Corinth

Cenchreae

Assos

Chios

Samos

Ephesus

Miletus

Cos

Rhodes

Patera

Myra

Iconium

Lystra

Derbe

Galatia

Pisidian
Antioch

Perga

Attalia

Paphos

Salamis

Seleucia

Antioch

Sidon

Tyre

Ptolemais

Caesarea

Antipatris

Jerusalem

First Journey
(Acts 13–14)

Second Journey
(Acts 15–18)

Third Journey
(Acts 18–21)

Fourth Journey
(Acts 23–end)

Proposed extension (Romans 15)

Letter Recipient

Good barber

THE PROBLEM OF MORALITY

Frankly, if you can explain Romans 7 then you're ahead of me on this one. But somewhere in there is the idea that we're often in conflict with ourselves, knowing what good we want to do, but somehow doing the opposite. While we might strive to change the picture, Paul would probably want to stress that divine grace is what really makes a difference. That and the fact that admin probably does have a moral dimension (1 Corinthians 12.28).

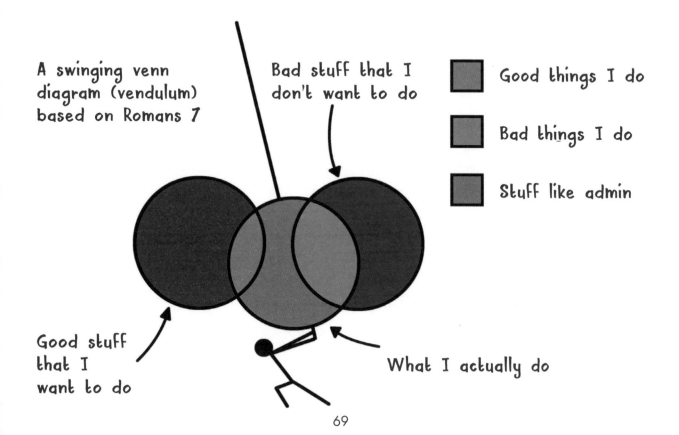

A swinging venn diagram (vendulum) based on Romans 7

Bad stuff that I don't want to do

Good things I do

Bad things I do

Stuff like admin

Good stuff that I want to do

What I actually do

PAUL'S THEOLOGY OF THE CROSS

Roman Corinth was an up-and-coming sort of place, where style, impressiveness and the latest ideas were all at the forefront of people's minds. Crashing right into that, Paul avoids trying to make Christ look even more impressive and focuses on the crucifixion, an embarrassment and failure by the standards of the day. Christ's cross seems to puncture human pomposity and self-aggrandisement. Here, it might be suggested that God has a track record of doing that.

Read about Balaam's donkey in Numbers 22.

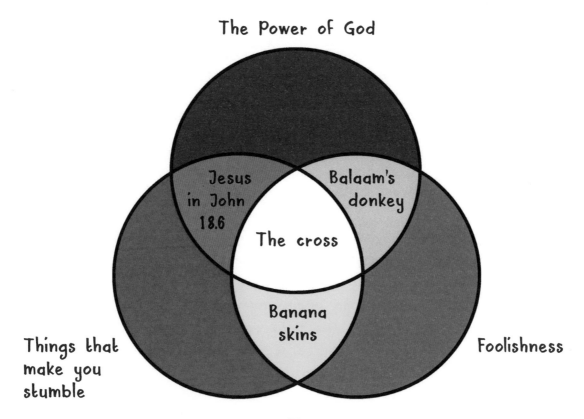

The Power of God

Jesus in John 18.6

Balaam's donkey

The cross

Banana skins

Things that make you stumble

Foolishness

THINGS PAUL KNEW WHEN FIRST COMING TO CORINTH
1 Corinthians 2.1-2

This is based on my own assumptions.

The point really follows on from the previous one, but it's interesting how often Paul appeals to his own story in his letters, as he does at this point. This could be mistaken for arrogance, but here at least he highlights just how weak a preacher he was in Corinth, again undercutting the Corinthians' culture of style over substance. Certainly this book could never be accused of putting style over substance, because of course, it has neither.

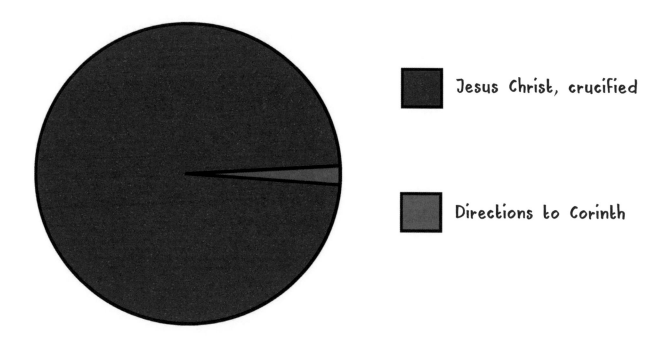

Jesus Christ, crucified

Directions to Corinth

1 CORINTHIANS 13 IN A NUTSHELL

Ever-popular at weddings, this passage was originally a fairly crucial point in Paul's debate with the Corinthians. It seems that they had become so excited by their new-found spiritual life that this excitement had eclipsed something that is more fundamental for Paul, namely love for one another. I suspect that this diagram will never be used in a wedding service, which is probably for the best, but it tries to capture Paul's basic argument. Using primary colours.

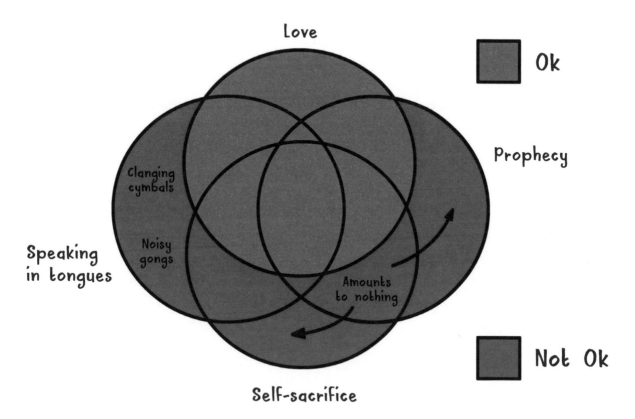

Love

Prophecy

Ok

Clanging cymbals

Noisy gongs

Amounts to nothing

Speaking in tongues

Not Ok

Self-sacrifice

75

PAUL DEFENDS HIS MINISTRY WITH A HANDY GRAPH

2 Corinthians 11

It's open to debate as to exactly who these super-apostles were, but Paul clearly senses that he has rivals. As noted above, Corinth was a prosperous, up-and-coming kind of place around this time, and people were on the lookout for impressive new ideas from impressive figures. So it's all the more striking that Paul abandons any attempt to appear relevant, arguing that his authority comes from his weakness. I don't know if there's anything we could learn from this today.

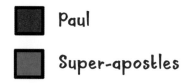

Paul

Super-apostles

Lots/high
quality

Not so
much/a
bit
rubbish

Quality of preaching | Quality of writing | Quality of service | Labours | Imprisonments | Floggings | Shipwrecks | Miscellaneous dangers

Apostleship: You do the math(s)

77

NEW TESTAMENT ESCHATOLOGY

We chatted earlier about how eschatology can refer to decisive moments in time. In the New Testament we find traces of the idea that Jesus' death and resurrection inaugurate the Kingdom of God. The Kingdom - the age to come - has begun in Christ, but the old world of evil continues for a time, though its eventual end is certain. That means that we live in the overlap of these two worlds.

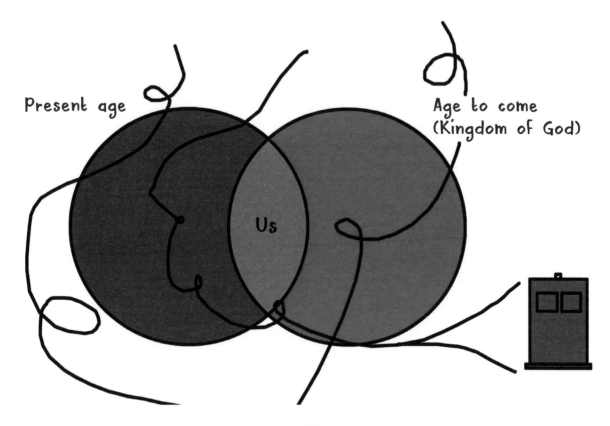

Present age

Age to come
(Kingdom of God)

Us

CREATION
Colossians 1

Some people have suggested that Colossians 1.15-20 and Philippians 2.6-11 (among others) are hymns that are either very early in origin or written by the author. Inevitably, some other people have suggested that they aren't. In this case, there is great beauty and rhythm in these verses, and that makes them worth savouring in their own right. But if you're in a hurry, the above diagram captures the gist of the first part at least.

Things in Heaven

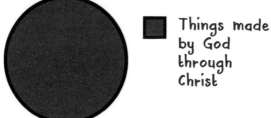

Things made by God through Christ

Things on Earth

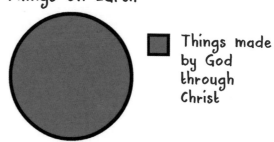

Things made by God through Christ

Things Visible

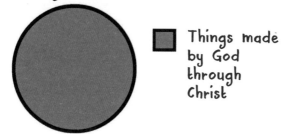

Things made by God through Christ

Things Invisible

Things made by God through Christ

FAITH AND WORKS

As it happens, there has been an awful lot of discussion about what Paul says on his own about faith and works, but this diagram is an attempt to make sense of the apparent contradiction between him and James. While I don't think we can completely iron out the differences (nor perhaps should we), the conflict is at least partly down to the fact that they begin from completely different points. Both would agree that faith is primary, and that action, growing from faith, is important. Or not. As you can see, it's a tricky one.

Paul

Works of the law

... all have sinned and fallen short ... (Romans 3.23)

... a person is justified by faith and not by works (Romans 3.28)

Do we then overthrow the law by this faith? By no means! On the contrary, we uphold the law (Romans 3.31)

Works of the law

Faith

James

Faith by itself, if it has no works, is dead (James 2.17)

... a person is justified by works and not by faith alone (James 2.24)

Faith

Works

Faith

I by my works will show you my faith (James 2.18)

A SIMPLE GUIDE TO THE LETTER OF JAMES

It's notoriously difficult to figure out the structure and exact purpose of James, so much so that some have suggested that it's no more than a random collection of thoughts. Chapter 1 works as an introduction to the rest of the letter/sermon. Beyond that, you're on your own a bit. What this diagram shows (sort of) is that these fragmented ideas do actually connect up, and that for the author the issues of poverty, speech, faith and works are all interconnected.

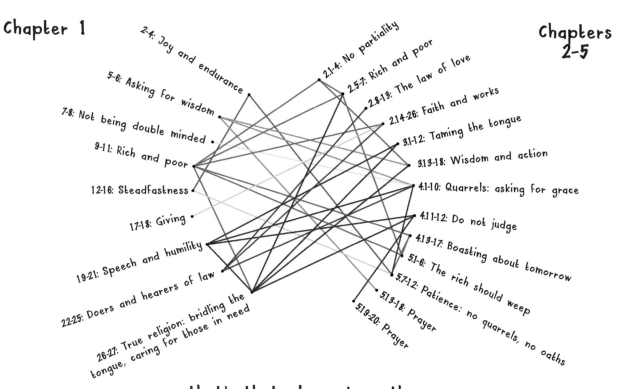

Chapter 1

2-4: Joy and endurance

2.1-4: No partiality

5-6: Asking for wisdom

2.5-7: Rich and poor

2.8-13: The law of love

7-8: Not being double minded

2.14-26: Faith and works

9-11: Rich and poor

3.1-12: Taming the tongue

3.13-18: Wisdom and action

12-16: Steadfastness

4.1-10: Quarrels: asking for grace

17-18: Giving

4.11-12: Do not judge

19-21: Speech and humility

4.13-17: Boasting about tomorrow

5.1-6: The rich should weep

22-25: Doers and hearers of law

5.7-12: Patience: no quarrels, no oaths

26-27: True religion: bridling the tongue, caring for those in need

5.13-18: Prayer

5.19-20: Prayer

... that's that cleared up then ...

THE SEVEN CHURCHES IN REVELATION 2–3

This one probably falls into the silly category, except that it raises an interesting question about the background to the book. It has often been stated that Revelation is directed to churches experiencing persecution, and some churches were certainly persecuted by the Roman Empire. But the letters suggest that some of the churches are complacent, and so perhaps need to do more to live differently. In this light, Revelation becomes a charge to stand up to the empire.

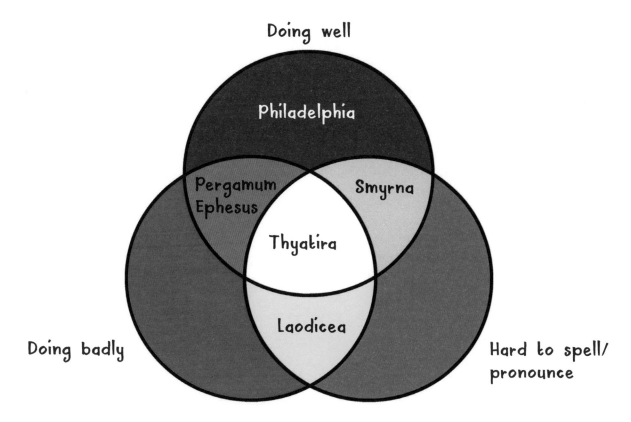

Doing well

Philadelphia

Pergamum
Ephesus

Smyrna

Thyatira

Laodicea

Doing badly

Hard to spell/
pronounce

AN APOCALYPTIC CHESS PUZZLE

Actually, this one belongs in the silly category.

Pestilence is limited to one quarter of the board. Utter chaos will ensue in three moves. What is the best move for John of Patmos?

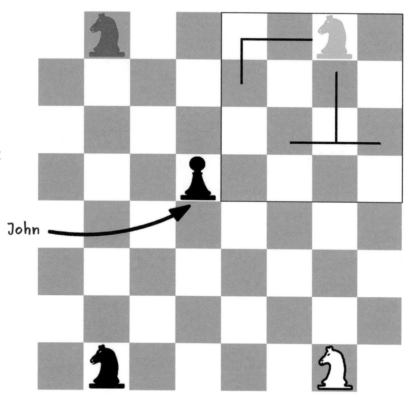

John

SOME WAYS TO INTERPRET REVELATION

Do the horses of Revelation 6 refer to historical figures, future events, or do they symbolise the oppression of Rome? Yes. Or no. This chart is designed to show what the options might be for interpreting such a difficult text. They're not completely exclusive - for example, a prediction of the literal end of the world could still be relevant to the first audience. Equally, you wouldn't have to take every passage as referring to the Roman Empire, even if you thought most of them were. Again, it's possible for a passage to refer to both a specific first-century event, whilst encapsulating some broader point. That's the genius of this genre. And the most dizzying aspect.

Mostly describes past events

	Yes ↓	No ↓	Maybe ↓
Yes →	**Preterist** the text refers to events around the time of writing, especially to do with the Roman empire	**Idealist** the text refers to timeless ideas, issues and principles	
No →	**Historicist** the text refers to events throughout history, with the last few still to come	**Futurist** the text refers to events mostly still to come, at the end of the world	
Maybe →			

Immediately applicable to first-century readers

The 'hedging your bets' approach

THE STRUCTURE OF REVELATION

I sometimes wished that the Bible just ended with a '... and they all lived happily ever after ...', though as the red line (preachability) suggests, that kind of happens at the end. What I think this diagram shows is that there is actually quite a lot of structure to this book (in fact much more than there is shown here), and that at least suggests that there is a lot more sense in the story than might first seem the case. For example, there are good reasons for thinking that the seals, trumpets and bowls are different images for the same thing, rather than events happening in sequence. In passing, the number 7 refers to the number of seals etc., and has less to do with preachability or the weather.

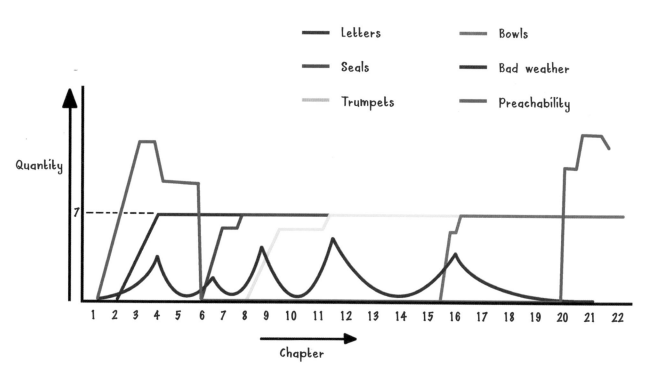

4
THE LIFE OF THE CHURCH

This section is somewhat influenced by my own Church tradition (Anglican) but I hope you are able to appreciate some of the things that transcend different denominations and things. The Anglican Church is a peculiar community of Christians who are united by their shared sense of being unsure about what we are. This makes us less coherent but hopefully more honest, at least to one another.

Most of these diagrams relate to things that go on in the life of the Church, but one or two are more serious (particularly the one about communion/ Holy Communion/the Eucharist/the Lord's table). In this case, I have avoided making any argument about what I think is correct, and instead have focused on simply charting the range of views. This is partly because that seems fairer, and also because I am eternally baffled about what I think is actually happening.

THE PRAYER OF PREPARATION

If you're not familiar with this one don't worry; it's a prayer that is used across several Church traditions to prepare people for sharing in communion. But more generally, you can see that it says something about God.

A time-saving chart

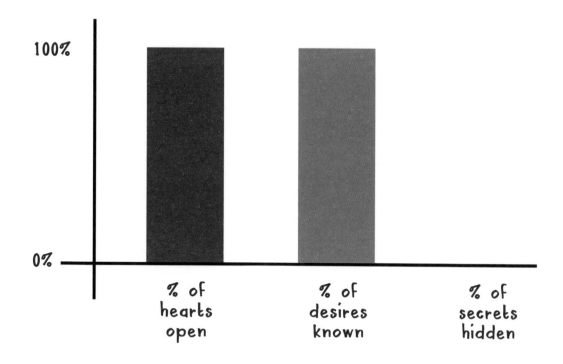

100%			
0%	% of hearts open	% of desires known	% of secrets hidden

MARKS OF MISSION

My own Church tradition suggested that there are five marks of mission, but honesty compels me to include six.

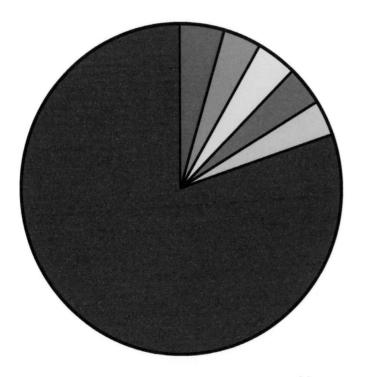

Proclaiming the Gospel

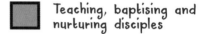
Teaching, baptising and
nurturing disciples

Caring for those in need

Challenging injustice,
pursuing peace

Protecting and sustaining
creation

Anxiety about talking to
other people

HOW TO REMEMBER WHEN ALL SAINTS' DAY IS

By now you may have deduced that I'm an Anglican, though don't let that put you off.

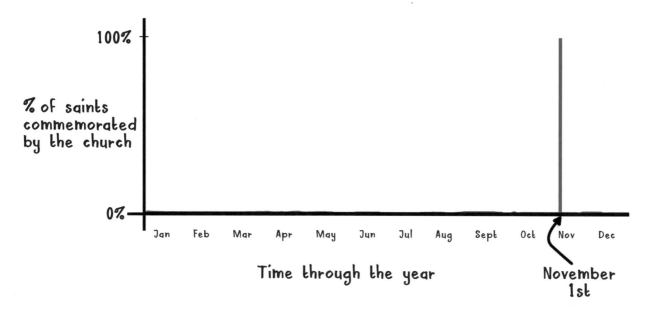

100%

% of saints
commemorated
by the church

0%

Jan Feb Mar Apr May Jun Jul Aug Sept Oct Nov Dec

Time through the year

November
1st

BREAKDOWN OF TIME SPENT DURING A HYMN

Yes, definitely Anglican.

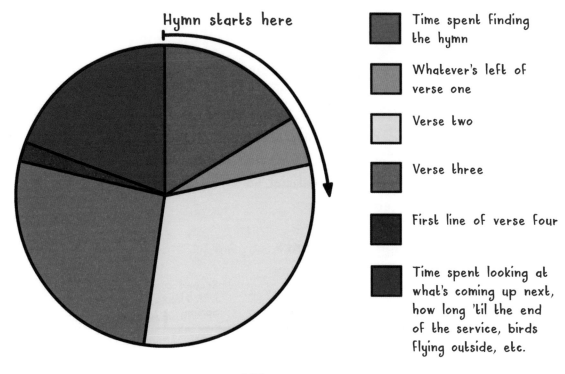

Hymn starts here

Time spent finding the hymn

Whatever's left of verse one

Verse two

Verse three

First line of verse four

Time spent looking at what's coming up next, how long 'til the end of the service, birds flying outside, etc.

VIEWS ON THE MILLENNIUM
Revelation 20.14

This could go in the New Testament section, except that it says more about Church history that this one passage of Revelation has created so much speculation. I have my own views about this, but I've never been clear as to why this level of debate would be beneficial to Christians. Shortbread, on the other hand, may be greatly edifying.

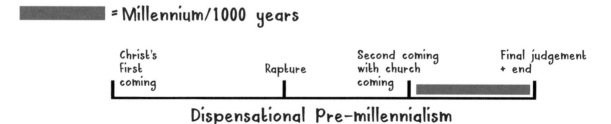

= Millennium/1000 years

Christ's first coming
Rapture
Second coming with church coming
Final judgement + end

Dispensational Pre-millennialism

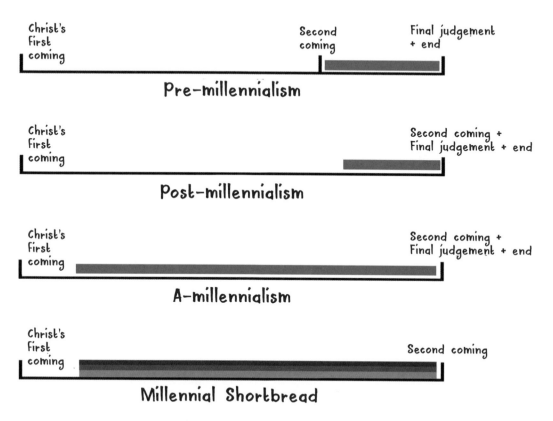

Christs
First
coming

Second
coming

Final judgement
+ end

Pre-millennialism

Christs
first
coming

Second coming +
Final judgement + end

Post-millennialism

Christs
first
coming

Second coming +
Final judgement + end

A-millennialism

Christs
first
coming

Second coming

Millennial Shortbread

MINISTRY IN THE CHURCH
Ephesians 4.11

Here, the more essential roles come lower, forming the foundations for the ones above.

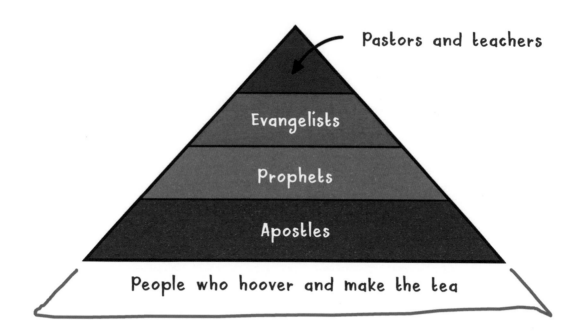

Pastors and teachers

Evangelists

Prophets

Apostles

People who hoover and make the tea

THE POST-SERVICE COFFEE AND BISCUITS

This may lead some people to question my commitment.

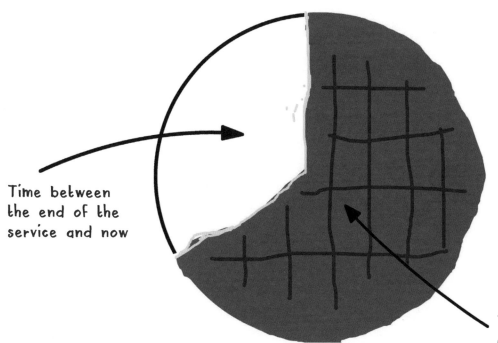

Time between
the end of the
service and now

Time from now
until I go home

BREAKDOWN OF TIME SPENT DURING A HYMN

(if you're the minister)

The only possible variation on this pie chart would be if the minister discovers that they have in fact announced the wrong hymn. There are a number of options in this scenario, but in the context of England where social embarrassment rules all, the preferred approach is to pretend that you have not noticed at all, and allow the organist to push on solo.

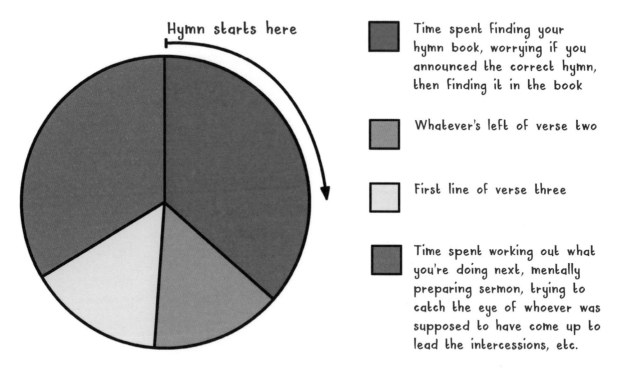

Hymn starts here

Time spent finding your hymn book, worrying if you announced the correct hymn, then finding it in the book

Whatever's left of verse two

First line of verse three

Time spent working out what you're doing next, mentally preparing sermon, trying to catch the eye of whoever was supposed to have come up to lead the intercessions, etc.

MINISTRY IN THE CHURCH
Corinthians 12.27-28

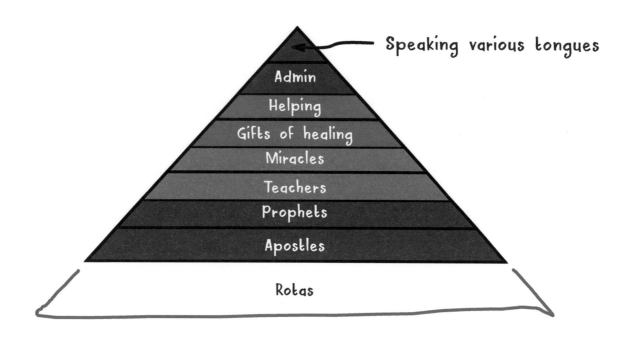

Speaking various tongues

Admin

Helping

Gifts of healing

Miracles

Teachers

Prophets

Apostles

Rotas

WHAT HAPPENS AT COMMUNION, I

I'm not going to get into the many complexities about what happens at communion. Well maybe a little. With Transubstantiation, the bread and wine change 'substance' but not 'accidents', which means that they stop being bread and wine but retain the appearance of bread and wine. In the Pneumatic view, the Holy Spirit takes the soul into heaven to encounter the body of Christ, so in a sense people are physically present to Christ. I told you it was complicated.

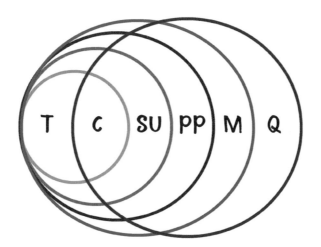

○ Christ is physically present in the bread and the wine

○ Christ is physically present

○ Christ is present through the Spirit

○ Christ is remembered

○ The bread and the wine remain bread and wine in substance

T = Transubstantiation
C = Consubstantiation
SU = Sacramental Union
PP = Pneumatic Presence
M = Memorialism
Q = Here, you are just having some bread and wine

WHAT HAPPENS AT COMMUNION, 2

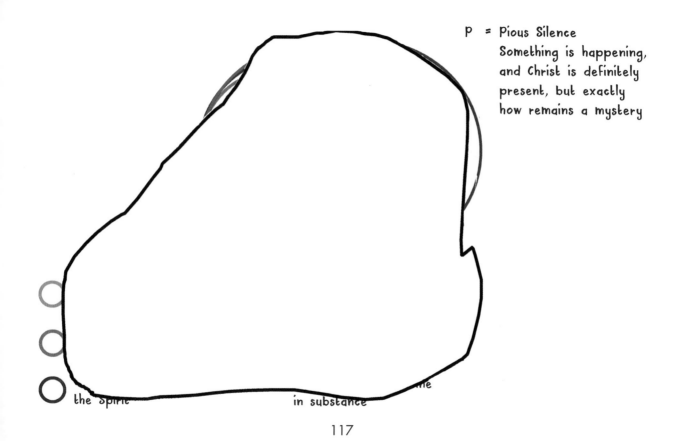

P = Pious Silence
Something is happening,
and Christ is definitely
present, but exactly
how remains a mystery

the Spirit

in substance

WHAT'S GOING ON IN THE MIND OF THE PERSON READING THE GOSPEL IN CHURCH

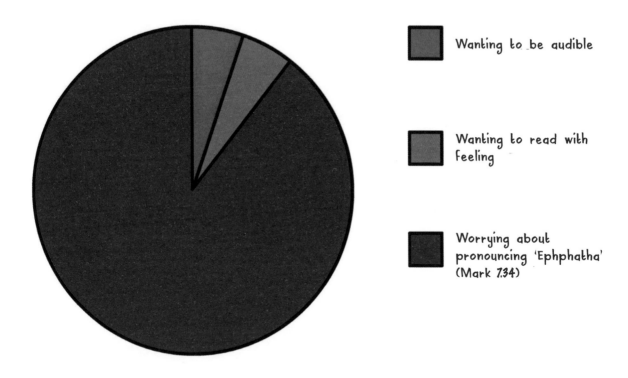

Wanting to be audible

Wanting to read with feeling

Worrying about pronouncing 'Ephphatha' (Mark 7.34)

WHAT PEOPLE TAKE AWAY FROM MY SERMONS

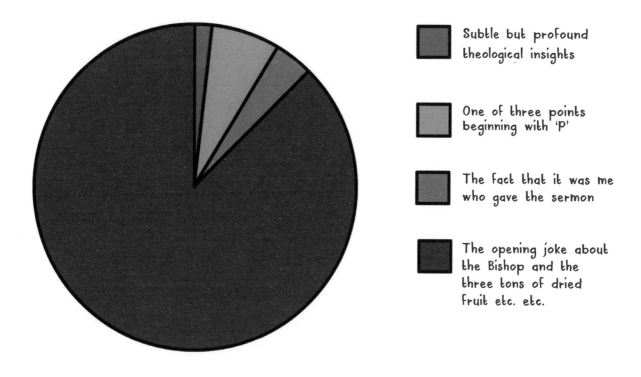

Subtle but profound theological insights

One of three points beginning with 'P'

The fact that it was me who gave the sermon

The opening joke about the Bishop and the three tons of dried fruit etc. etc.

5
THEOLOGY

'What is theology?' I hear you ask. Not that I'm listening in to your thoughts I should add. It's an important and difficult question, one that this section of the book will do almost nothing to answer. But I think that there are perhaps good reasons for not worrying too much about defining theology. My own view is that the subject of theology (God) is too big to be contained by a carefully defined human enterprise, and so in practice theology is quite a diverse range of things which cluster around the idea of knowing God. If this is right, then two ideas stick out for me. One, theology is about loving God with the mind (Luke 10.27). Two, theology is about being transformed by the renewal of the mind (Romans 12.2). To be fair, you might take a different view, and that's just hunky dory.

Anyway, what follows are a set of diagrams which include things to do with ethics, with our understanding of God, Christ, life after death, and our understanding of understanding. That last one is as fun as it sounds.

AUGUSTINE ON SCRIPTURE

Among quite a lot of other things, Augustine argued that one of the main purposes of scripture was to build up love in its readers. If a person misunderstood a passage but still grew in love, it was far better than if they had 'got it right' but not grown in love. I shall attempt to use this idea to cover over any inaccuracies in this book.

What can I say about Augustine? Not a lot, mainly owing to ignorance on my part. He was Bishop of Hippo in North Africa, and one of the most influential thinkers and writers of the early Church. Augustine has recently found favour again among thinkers who want to maintain that the Bible should be read for theology and devotion, and not only as a historical source, a perspective which has been prominent among biblical scholarship. But that's a much longer story for another day.

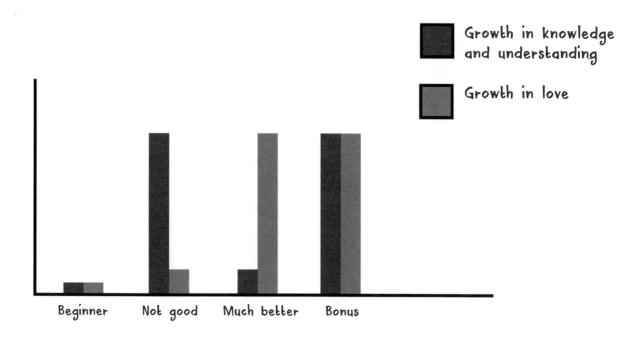

Beginner Not good Much better Bonus

Growth in knowledge and understanding

Growth in love

THE VENERABLE BEDE

In his Ecclesiastical History, Bede seems particularly concerned about whether or not people keep Easter on the correct day, and whether or not monks had the correct tonsure (haircut) (in the shape of a crown) (there are too many brackets in this sentence). Weirdly, this may not have been a big issue in Bede's day, though it had certainly been not long before. It's interesting how divisions in the Church, which seem so important at the time, can seem so peculiar from another perspective. Again, I don't know if there's anything we could take away from this.

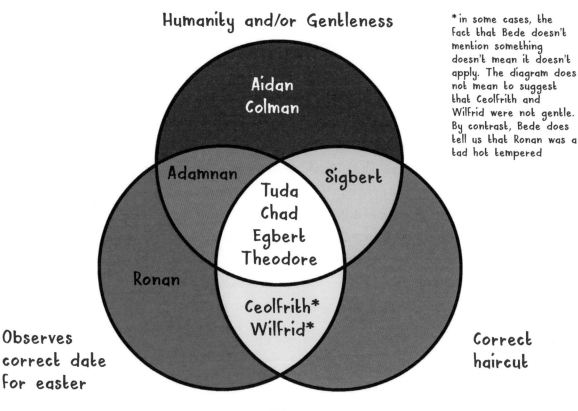

Humanity and/or Gentleness

Aidan
Colman

Adamnan

Sigbert

Tuda
Chad
Egbert
Theodore

Ronan

Ceolfrith*
Wilfrid*

Observes
correct date
for easter

Correct
haircut

*in some cases, the
fact that Bede doesn't
mention something
doesn't mean it doesn't
apply. The diagram does
not mean to suggest
that Ceolfrith and
Wilfrid were not gentle.
By contrast, Bede does
tell us that Ronan was a
tad hot tempered

THE EARLIEST THEOLOGYGRAM?

Diagram A dates back at least as far as the thirteenth century and proves, if nothing else, that someone else had the idea behind this book first. The diagram sets out the idea that each person of the Trinity is fully God yet distinct from the other persons. The other two diagrams are more recent, and set out a couple of pitfalls in Trinitarian theology. In (B), each actor is distinct, but they come in sequence, and are not simultaneously Dr Who (except when they are in special episodes). In (C), Jeff is simultaneously three distinct 'persons', but the three roles can't really relate to each other as persons. I think my point is that diagram (A) is helpful, but there is probably more to be said about the Trinity than you can fit into a diagram.

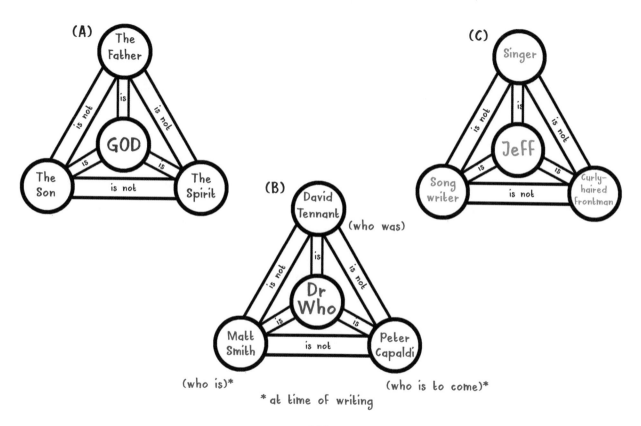

(A)

The Father

is

GOD

is not — is not

is — is

The Son — is not — The Spirit

(B)

David Tennant (who was)

is

Dr Who

is not — is not

is — is

Matt Smith — is not — Peter Capaldi

(who is)*

(who is to come)*

* at time of writing

(C)

Singer

is

Jeff

is not — is not

is — is

Song writer — is not — Curly-haired frontman

THE INCARNATIONAL WASHING-LINE

It's easy to imagine that big concepts like the Trinity or the incarnation were plucked out of thin air (or at least divinely revealed out of the blue). However, I think they're more like an attempt to make sense of important ideas that are hard to fit together. So the idea of the incarnation emerged from the conviction that Jesus was fully human, yet somehow also fully God. These two beliefs are hard to fit together, they don't seem to 'touch'; even so, they create a tension which is essential to keeping the theological washing up.

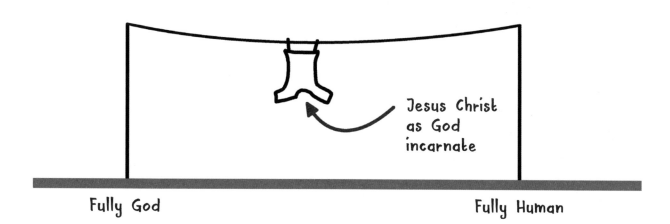

Fully God

Fully Human

Jesus Christ as God incarnate

SOME COMMON APPROACHES TO DOING THEOLOGY

Sometimes theology seems completely unrelated to real life. Here are three suggestions for how it could be. Version A (The Pastoral Cycle) is actually used by people who do theology. Version B on the other hand ... well it's hard to say whether or not we do this. Jeremiah is issuing a sustained plea for the people to return to the way of God. It comes in the midst of some pretty difficult warnings, but perhaps it contains an urgency that's worth taking on board. If theology seems like a very detached and academic discipline, Jeremiah might remind us that in a world of great suffering there is an urgent need to seek God for the sake of the world.

I may be over-reaching myself on this point. Don't let my sermonising put you off.

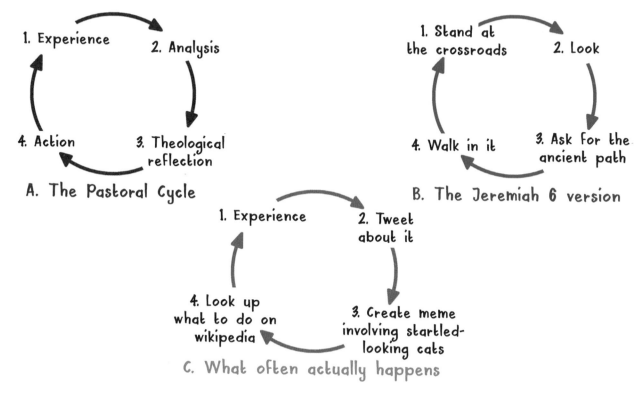

1. Experience
2. Analysis
3. Theological reflection
4. Action

A. The Pastoral Cycle

1. Stand at the crossroads
2. Look
3. Ask for the ancient path
4. Walk in it

B. The Jeremiah 6 version

1. Experience
2. Tweet about it
3. Create meme involving startled-looking cats
4. Look up what to do on wikipedia

C. What often actually happens

THE TRINITARIAN WASHING-LINE

As noted, the Trinity can create a bit of a theological pickle. As before, this diagram doesn't explain it, but suggests that there are two basic convictions that are worth holding on to, even if they seem difficult to reconcile.

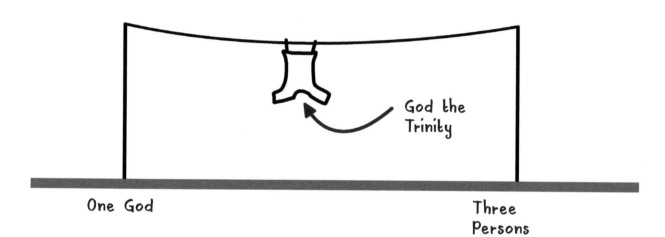

One God

Three Persons

God the Trinity

TRACING THE WISDOM TRADITIONS

Job asks, 'Where shall wisdom be found?' Here are some suggestions.

	Proverbs	Jesus	James	Mr T
Counsels the foolish	✓ (Pr. 8.5) →	✓ (Luke 11.40, 24.25) →	✓ (James 1.5-8, 2.20) →	✓
Respects mothers	✓ (Pr. 23.22, 23.25, 30.17) →	✓ (John 19.26-27) —————→		✓
Dislikes gold	✓ (Pr. 8.10, 8.19, 16.16.) →	✓ (Matthew 23.17) →	✓ (James 2.2, 5.3)	
Advocates the cessation of jibber-jabber	✓ (Pr. 10.19, 11.12) →	✓ (Matthew 6.7) →	✓ (James 1.19, 1.26, 3.1-12) →	✓

IMMORTALITY VERSUS RESURRECTION

Here are two ways that people have traditionally thought about life after death. In the first one, human beings have a spiritual part and a physical part. When the physical body dies, the spiritual bit, which is immortal, lives on with God. While this sounds a bit like what Paul says in 1 Corinthians 15, I'd like briefly to nail some colours to the theological mast and advocate the second option for two reasons. Firstly, while some ancient philosophers had thought that the physical world was evil, a lot of scripture talks about the goodness of creation, and the goodness of the physical world. Secondly, the idea of resurrection has less to do with human capabilities, and more to do with a gift of God. Resurrection speaks of God's faithfulness beyond death.

Immortality of the soul

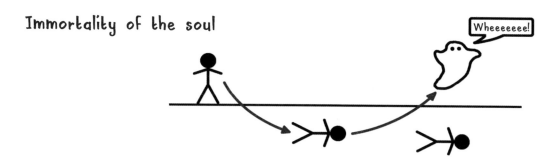

Resurrection of the body

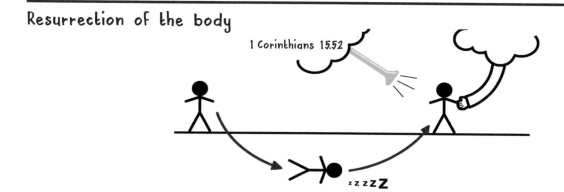

CHALLENGES OF BIBLE TRANSLATION

Because of the way language works, there's really no such thing as a 'correct' translation, so Bible translators have to weigh up various ideals. On the one hand, being as accurate as possible is a good thing, but following the original language too literally will lead to very peculiar English. So on the other hand, it's good to come up with English that mirrors how people actually speak and write – this is the search for 'dynamic equivalence'. This is a bit of an art, as sometimes a great sounding English phrase might take a few too many liberties with the originals....

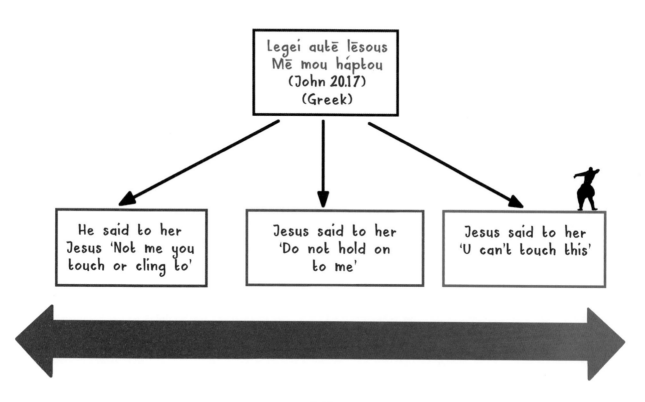

HERESY FOR BEGINNERS

It's probably a bit unfair to throw in some obscure words with no explanation. Not only that, but words like 'heresy' can seem pretty harsh, especially when a lot of it comes down to attempts to make sense of something quite mysterious. In this tiny paragraph, I would say that it can be helpful to think through what is at stake when trying to make sense of a question like 'Who was Jesus?' Often the most important things are time, perspective and five portions of fruit and veg per day. The latter won't help with theology, but it's probably a good idea.

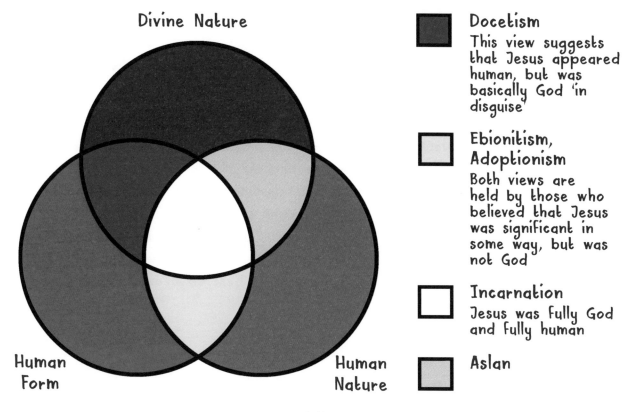

Divine Nature

Human Form

Human Nature

Docetism
This view suggests that Jesus appeared human, but was basically God 'in disguise'

Ebionitism, Adoptionism
Both views are held by those who believed that Jesus was significant in some way, but was not God

Incarnation
Jesus was fully God and fully human

Aslan

FOUR MAJOR APPROACHES TO ETHICS

Here are four (well, three in reality) different ways of thinking about ethics. Each has numerous variants, and they are not necessarily incompatible with one another; indeed most of the time we probably think with a mixture of these perspectives. The advantage of distinguishing them is that when a disagreement occurs, it can be helpful to think about whether we're asking different kinds of questions to our companions, and in turn this can help us to see it from another angle. Unless that angle involves conquering the galaxy. If that's what your companions are arguing for, it's best to beat a hasty retreat.

	Focuses on	Considers	... in terms of ...	Typical question
Deontological Ethics	Duty	Action	... what is right	What is the right thing to do regardless of the result?
Teleological Ethics (sometimes Consequentialism)	Outcomes	Action	... what is good	What action leads to the best result for the most people?
Virtue Ethics	Character	Persons	... who I ought to be to achieve good ends	Which characteristic traits lead to good living?
	Extermination	Exterminating things	... how best to exterminate as many things as possible	How can I exterminate more things?

APOPHATIC THEOLOGY

Apophatic and cataphatic are not words that I would recommend using at a dinner party/in a sermon/ever, but if you've ever felt like you couldn't find the words to describe God, then this one is for you. Someone pointed out that when we say God is love (for example), our understanding of what that means is limited by our experience of love. God's love goes beyond human words.

So apophatic (or negative) theology is all about saying what God is not. Or you might say apophatic theology is not about saying what God is. Or it's not saying what God is about.

Cataphatic Theology

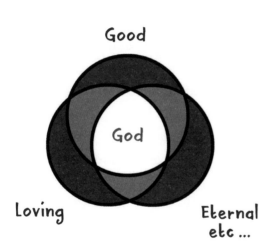

Good

Loving

God

Eternal
etc ...

Apophatic Theology

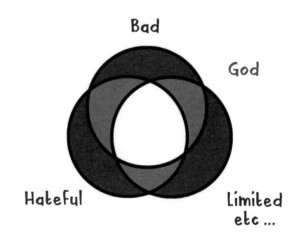

Bad

God

Hateful

Limited
etc ...

This diagram has no jokes due to cutbacks

KARL BARTH'S DIALECTICAL WASHING-LINE

Ok, apophatic theology is not about not saying what God is not about. Anyway, the twentieth-century theologian Karl Barth was well aware that we could never really find the right words to describe God, but he also believed that it was essential to try for the sake of good preaching. This creates another washing-line situation: preachers should not give up, but nor should they presume that they've got it right. Both poles of the washing-line are worth holding on to.

Karl Barth (1886-1968) was a Swiss theologian whose work was hugely influential, not least the enormous and unfinished CHURCH DOGMATICS. He is notable for reacting against various strands of theology which he felt had little to say in the face of the horrors of the First World War, and went on to articulate opposition to the collusion of many Churches with Nazism. He also smoked a pipe.

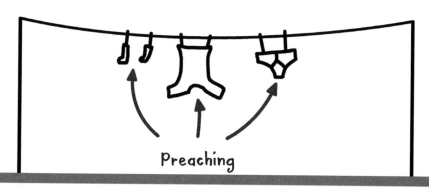

Preaching

Impossibility of finding
words adequate to
speak of God

Necessity of
speaking to God

JUST WAR CHECKLIST

The just war tradition goes back at least as far as Augustine. It has evolved over the years, so this chart only shows a snapshot of a much bigger tradition. The upper section describes questions about whether or not it is right to go into war, while the lower section contains questions about appropriate conduct during war. The final score is a bit of a red herring because, in reality, these criteria aren't boxes that can be ticked off; deciding whether or not they have been met is far more complicated than that. As a result, you may well disagree with my conclusions, and so I've included a blank table below for your own use.

		STAR WARS Rebels vs. Death Star	DOCTOR WHO: Dalek campaigns	Harry Potter vs. Voldemort and co	LORD OF THE RINGS: Final Battle	INDEPENDENCE DAY: Humans vs. Aliens
Just decision to go to war (Jus ad bellum)	A) Is the purpose just?	✓		✓	✓	✓
	B) Is there legitimate authority to declare war?	✓	✓	?	✓	✓
	C) Will the war be fought with good intentions?	✓		✓	✓	
	D) Is this war the last resort?	✓		✓	✓	
	E) Are the expected effects of the war proportionate?			✓	✓	
	F) Is there a reasonable expectation of success?		✓			
Just conduct in war (Jus in bello)	A) Discrimination: are civilians being avoided?	✓		✓	✓	✓
	B) Proportionality: is the use of force proportionate to a just outcome?			Tricky with magic	✓	
	C) Legality: are the rights of the opposing forces being honoured?			✓	?	
Round-up	Final Score	**5**	**2**	**6**	**6**	**3**
	Notes	Skywalker: Man of the match for trying to save Vader		Potter: Yellow card for excessive shouting at enemies		

DIY JUST WAR CHECKLIST

P.S. The other question is whether or not the just war criteria are correct in the first place. Christianity has a strong parallel tradition of pacifism, which also goes back a very long way.

Just decision to go to war (Jus ad bellum)	A) Is the purpose just?					
	B) Is there legitimate authority to declare war?					
	C) Will the war be fought with good intentions?					
	D) Is this war the last resort?					
	E) Are the expected effects of the war proportionate?					
	F) Is there a reasonable expectation of success?					
Just conduct in war (Jus in bello)	A) Discrimination: are civilians being avoided?					
	B) Proportionality: is the use of force proportionate to a just outcome?					
	C) Legality: are the rights of the opposing forces being honoured?					
Round-up	Final Score					
	Notes					

THE HERMENEUTICAL CIRCLE

Hermeneutics is simply the study of how we go from reading something to making sense of it. If I read John's Gospel, for example, my understanding of the whole book is built up from my understanding of each part, even each individual word. But equally, my understanding of a word like 'love' is shaped by my understanding of the whole book, because the book as a whole gives us a picture of what love looks like. Hopefully, as I reread it my understanding of both the whole story, and of each part, will grow. This process is known as the hermeneutical circle.

1. The Hermeneutical Circle

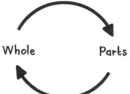

Whole   Parts

The whole text makes sense of the parts, the parts make sense of the whole

2. The Hermeneutical Spiral

Whole   Parts

As the circle repeats, under-standing grows

3. The Hermeneutical Catherine Wheel

Whole   Parts

As the circle repeats, the mind is dist Look a kitten!

4. The Hermeneutical Turntable

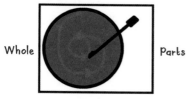

Whole   Parts

Sometimes understanding decreases until the reader goes round and round and ...

5. The Hermeneutical Roundabout (Marxist)

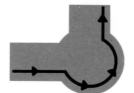

Give way to opinions from the left

6. The Hermeneutical Mini Roundabout

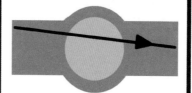

MY INTERPRETATION IS CORRECT!

REVELATION AND/OR NATURAL LAW

Looking at it again, I'm not convinced this diagram helps matters. The question is whether or not being created by God means that all humanity has the ability to work out what is morally right through human reason. In favour of this idea, natural law people point out that humans are made in God's image and have therefore been given the capacity to do moral thinking. Against this, revelation people suggest that sin corrupts our ability to think unselfishly, so we need the grace of God. As usual, there are actually many variations on this theme.

Revelation-based ethics

GOD

HUMAN KIND

Natural law ethics

GOD

CREATION   HUMAN KIND

What doing ethics often feels like

GOD

OTHER OPINIONS

CREATION   HUMAN KIND

QUESTIONS I ASK WHEN READING SCRIPTURE

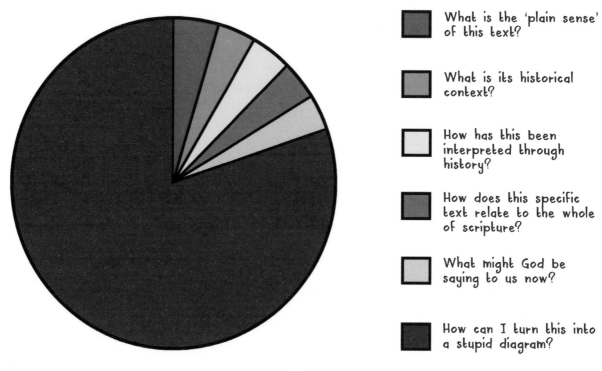

What is the 'plain sense' of this text?

What is its historical context?

How has this been interpreted through history?

How does this specific text relate to the whole of scripture?

What might God be saying to us now?

How can I turn this into a stupid diagram?